This book was purchased with
a grant from the
ABC/25 Foundation.
2003-2004

Oceans and Seas

Caribbean Sea

John F. Prevost
ABDO Publishing Company

visit us at
www.abdopub.com

Published by ABDO Publishing Company, 4940 Viking Drive, Edina, Minnesota 55435.
Copyright © 2003 by Abdo Consulting Group, Inc. International copyrights reserved in
all countries. No part of this book may be reproduced in any form without written
permission from the publisher.

Printed in the United States.

Photo Credits: Corbis

Contributing Editors: Kate A. Conley, Kristin Van Cleaf, Kristianne E. Vieregger
Art Direction & Maps: Neil Klinepier

Library of Congress Cataloging-in-Publication Data

Prevost, John F.
    Caribbean Sea / John F. Prevost.
        p. cm. -- (Oceans and seas)
    Includes index.
    Summary: Surveys the origin, geological borders, climate, water, plant and animal
 life, and economic and ecological aspects of the Caribbean Sea.
    ISBN 1-57765-096-4
    1. Caribbean Sea--Juvenile literature. [1. Caribbean Sea.] I. Title. II. Series:
Prevost, John F. Oceans and seas.
GC531.P74 1999
551.46'35--dc21   98-12654
                                                                         CIP
                                                                          AC

Contents

The Caribbean Sea

What do hurricanes, manatees, and mangrove trees have in common? They are all parts of the Caribbean **Sea**! This body of water is part of the Atlantic Ocean. Its warm, clear water covers about 1 million square miles (3 million sq km).

Groups of islands called the Greater Antilles and the Lesser Antilles are in the Caribbean Sea. These island groups form the boundary between the Caribbean Sea and the Atlantic Ocean. Central America and South America make up the Caribbean Sea's other boundaries.

The Caribbean Sea is connected to many bodies of water. The Yucatán Channel links the Caribbean Sea to the Gulf of Mexico. Straits, such as the Windward Passage and the Mona Passage, join the Caribbean Sea with the Atlantic Ocean. Farther south, the Panama Canal connects the Caribbean Sea to the Pacific Ocean.

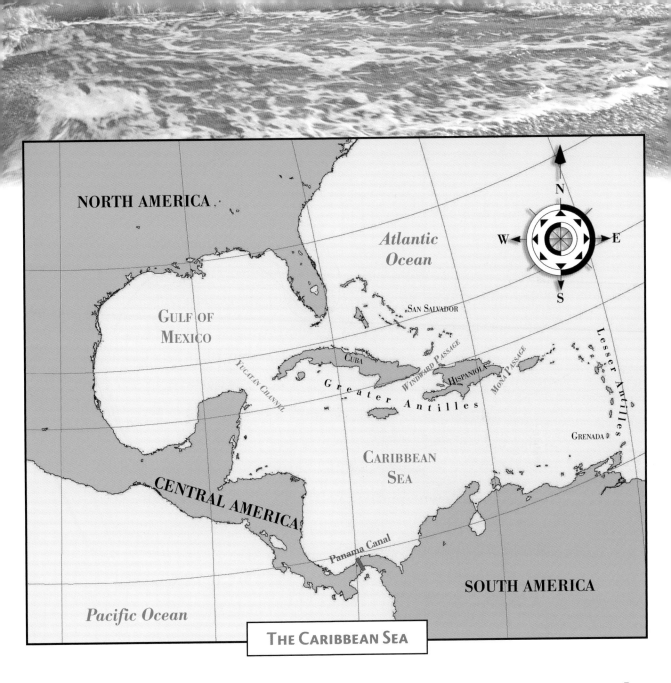

NORTH AMERICA

Atlantic Ocean

N

W   E

S

GULF OF MEXICO

San Salvador

CUBA

*Y*ucatan *Channel*

Windward Passage

Hispaniola

Mona Passage

Lesser Antilles

Greater Antilles

CARIBBEAN SEA

Grenada

CENTRAL AMERICA

Panama Canal

SOUTH AMERICA

Pacific Ocean

THE CARIBBEAN SEA

Forming the Sea

Scientists believe that millions of years ago, Earth had only one continent, Pangaea. It was surrounded by one ocean, Panthalassa. Over time, Pangaea broke apart. The pieces formed today's continents, dividing Panthalassa into smaller oceans and **seas**, such as the Caribbean.

The Caribbean's seafloor is made up of the Yucatán, Cayman, Colombian, Venezuelan, and Grenada Basins. Each basin is roughly shaped like an O. Underwater ridges and rises separate the basins from each other.

Trenches are also found on the Caribbean's seafloor. The Cayman Trench is 25,216 feet (7,686 m) deep. This makes it the deepest point in the Caribbean Sea. Earthquakes are common around the edges of this trench.

The Caribbean Sea also has underwater volcanoes. One of the best-known is Kick-'em-Jenny. It is located near the island of Grenada. Kick-'em-Jenny has erupted several times in the past 60 years.

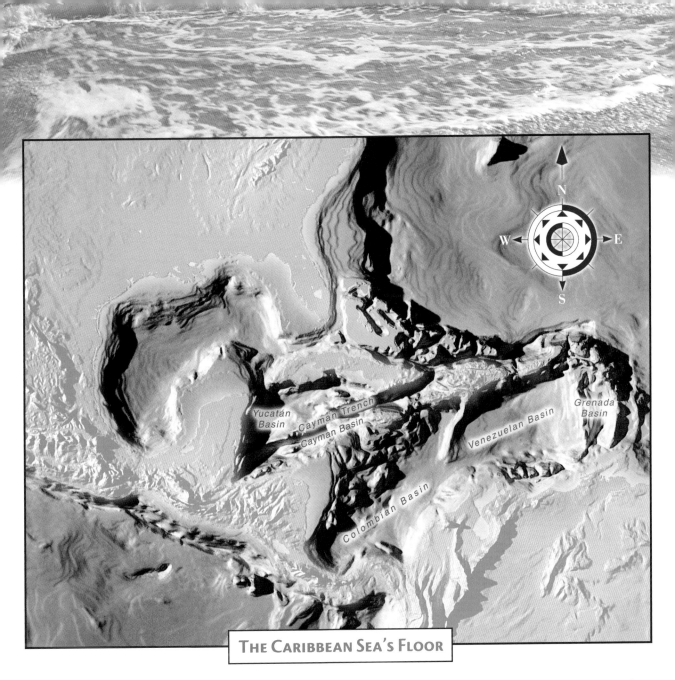

Yucatán Basin

Cayman Trench

Cayman Basin

Venezuelan Basin

Grenada Basin

Colombian Basin

N
W E
S

THE CARIBBEAN SEA'S FLOOR

The Caribbean's Water

Water from the Atlantic Ocean enters the Caribbean **Sea** near the Lesser Antilles. The water forms the Caribbean Current. A current is a strong stream moving within a larger body of water.

The Caribbean Current flows northwest. It moves at a rate of 15 to 17 inches (38 to 43 cm) per second. Eventually, the current passes through the Yucatán Channel. There, it forms part of the **Gulf Stream**.

The Caribbean Sea's water is very clear. In some places, it is possible to see more than 200 feet (61 m) below the surface. The water is clear because it doesn't contain much **plankton**.

The Caribbean's water is also very warm. In the summer, the water's temperature can reach 83°F (28°C). The warm water temperature occurs because the Caribbean Sea is located near the **equator**.

The Caribbean's warm, clear water makes it a great place for divers.

Climate

The Caribbean **Sea** and its islands have a **tropical** climate. This climate has two seasons. One season is rainy, and the other is dry. During both seasons, the air is often **humid**. Temperatures are between 70 and 80°F (21 and 27°C).

The trade winds affect the Caribbean's climate. These winds blow westward over Earth's tropical regions. When the trade winds blow over the Caribbean Sea, they bring rain. The heaviest rain falls on the **windward sides** of the islands.

Tropical storms called hurricanes are another major part of the Caribbean's climate. Hurricanes have heavy rain, lightning, thunder, and winds faster than 74 miles per hour (119 km/h). A hurricane has the power to destroy whatever is in its path.

Opposite page: The sunny shore of the Caribbean Sea

Hurricanes form in the eastern Atlantic Ocean. Then they follow the same path as the trade winds. Each year, the Caribbean experiences about eight hurricanes. Most occur between June and November.

Plants

Many kinds of plants grow in the Caribbean **Sea**. Sea grasses often grow near coral **reefs**. Some common Caribbean sea grasses include turtle grass, manatee grass, and shoal grass. They provide food and shelter for many sea animals.

Plants called algae also grow in the Caribbean. Some types of algae produce **limestone**. When these plants die, the limestone **erodes** and forms sand. Over time, this process has created the Caribbean's white sand beaches.

Red and black mangrove trees grow along the Caribbean's shore. They have adapted to living near salt water. Their roots grow above ground, protecting the shore from erosion. Mangrove swamps are home to birds, snakes, and crocodiles.

Coconut palm trees also grow along the sandy shores of the Caribbean Sea. They grow to be about 80 feet (24 m) tall. Each year, they produce coconuts, which can be eaten raw or dried for later use.

A puffer fish swims in a bed of turtle grass in the Caribbean Sea.

Animals

Coral are some of the Caribbean **Sea**'s best-known animals. They live in colonies in warm, shallow water. When coral die, they leave behind hard skeletons. Over hundreds of years, the coral skeletons form **reefs**.

A conch

The Caribbean's Mesoamerican Reef is the largest coral reef of the Americas. It stretches for nearly 450 miles (724 km) near the coasts of Mexico, Belize, Honduras, and Guatemala. It is home to many animals, including more than 500 fish species.

Other interesting animals live in the Caribbean Sea, too. Manta rays are fish that glide through the water using long, wide fins. Queen

*The Caribbean Sea's reefs are full
of colorful plants and animals.*

conchs are snails that live in the **sea**. Their large, spiral shells can grow to be one foot (30 cm) long!

Some of the Caribbean's animals are in danger from human activities. Some of these animals include manatees, sea turtles, and crocodiles. They have been hurt by pollution, hunting, and loss of **habitat**.

The First Settlers

For years, people have lived on the islands in the Caribbean **Sea**. These peoples formed three different groups. They were the Arawak, the Ciboney, and the Carib.

The Arawak was the largest group. They settled in the Greater Antilles. The Arawak grew crops, hunted, and fished. They also built large villages. Some of the villages had about 3,000 people.

The Ciboney also lived in the Greater Antilles. They lived in caves and small settlements along the Caribbean's shore. Over time, the Arawak forced the Ciboney to remote areas on the islands of Hispaniola and Cuba.

The Caribs settled in the Lesser Antilles. They were warriors. The Caribs traveled the sea in dugout canoes to raid other native villages. The Caribbean Sea was later named after the Carib people.

A Carib father makes a model of a dugout canoe for his son.

Exploration

European exploration of the Caribbean **Sea** and its islands began in 1492. That year, Christopher Columbus began exploring the region. Columbus was an Italian explorer who worked for Spain's king and queen.

Columbus reached a **cay** just north of the Caribbean Sea in October 1492. He named the cay San Salvador. Columbus took possession of San Salvador in the name of Spain.

Then Columbus traveled farther south. He discovered the Caribbean island called Hispaniola. There, he established a successful Spanish colony.

Soon, other Spanish explorers claimed many of the other Caribbean islands. The Spaniards used native peoples as slaves to mine for gold and other metals. This difficult work killed nearly all of the natives on the islands.

British, French, and Dutch explorers soon claimed islands in the Caribbean, too. Then the Europeans established sugar plantations. They used slaves from Africa to do the plantation work.

Christopher Columbus and his crew land on San Salvador in 1492.

The Caribbean Today

The Caribbean **Sea** has many resources. Fishers catch lobsters, queen conchs, sardines, and tuna from the Caribbean Sea. Ships travel on the sea to transport products from the Caribbean to other parts of the world.

The Caribbean's warm, sunny weather and beautiful beaches are also important resources. They attract tourists from around the world. Tourism has become a major part of the economy for many Caribbean islands.

Tourists enjoy spending time in the Caribbean Sea.

Fishers from the Dominican Republic haul in their day's catch.

Today, many nations are working to protect the Caribbean's resources. In 1997, Mexico, Belize, Honduras, and Guatemala signed the Tulum Declaration. They agreed to work together to protect the Mesoamerican **Reef**. With efforts such as this, the Caribbean will be a healthy, beautiful **sea** for years to come.

Glossary

cay - a low island or reef made of sand or coral.

equator - an imaginary circle around the middle of Earth. The region near the equator has a warm climate.

erode - to wash or wear away.

Gulf Stream - a swift, warm current in the North Atlantic Ocean. It warms the land it passes.

habitat - a place where a certain living thing is naturally found.

humid - moisture or dampness in the air.

limestone - a rock that is made up of calcium carbonate.

plankton - small plants and animals that float in a body of water.

reef - a chain of rocks or coral, or a ridge of sand, near the water's surface.

sea - a body of water that is smaller than an ocean and is almost completely surrounded by land.

tropical - a climate that doesn't get frost. Tropical climates are warm enough to grow plants all year long.

windward side - the side facing the direction from which the wind blows. For example, when the wind is blowing from the west, the western side of an island is the windward side.

How Do You Say That?

algae - AL-jee
Antilles - an-TIH-leez
Arawak - AIR-uh-wahk
Carib - KAIR-uhb
Caribbean - kair-uh-BEE-uhn
cay - KEE

Ciboney - see-buh-NAY
conch - KAHNGK
Hispaniola - hihs-puhn-YO-luh
Pangaea - pan-JEE-uh
Panthalassa - pan-THA-luh-suh
Yucatán - yoo-kah-TAHN

Web Sites

Would you like to learn more about the Caribbean Sea? Please visit **www.abdopub.com** to find up-to-date Web site links about the Caribbean Sea and its creatures. These links are routinely monitored and updated to provide the most current information available.

Index